HONEY

HONEY

southwater

This edition published by Southwater

Distributed in the UK by
The Manning Partnership
Batheaston, Bath BA1 7RL, UK
tel. (0044) 01225 852 727
fax. (0044) 01225 852 852

Distributed in the USA by
Ottenheimer Publishing
5 Park Center Court
Suite 300
Owing Mills MD 2117-5001, USA
tel. (001) 410 902 9100
fax. (001) 410 902 7210

Distributed in Australia by
Sandstone Publishing
56 John Street, Leichhardt
New South Wales 2040, Australia
tel. (0061) 2 9552 3815
fax. (0061) 2 9552 1538

Distributed in New Zealand by
Five Mile Press NZ
Unit 3/46a Taharoto Road, PO Box 33-1071
Takapuna, Auckland 9, New Zealand
tel. (0064) 9 486 1925
fax. (0064) 9 486 1454

Southwater is an imprint of
Anness Publishing Limited
© 1997, 2000 Anness Publishing Limited
1 3 5 7 9 10 8 6 4 2

Publisher: Joanna Lorenz
Senior Cookery Editor: Linda Fraser
Cookery Editor: Anne Hildyard
Designer: Bill Mason
Illustrations: Anna Koska

Photographers: Steve Baxter, James Duncan, Michelle Garrett, Nelson Hargreaves, Amanda Heywood, David Jordan,
Don Last, Patrick McLeavey and Thomas Odulate
Recipes: Alex Barker, Kit Chan, Carole Clements, Christine France, Sarah Gates, Sue Maggs,
Liz Trigg and Pamela Westland
Food for photography: Carla Capalbo, Carole Handslip, Wendy Lee,
Jane Stevenson and Elizabeth Wolf-Cohen
Stylists: Madeleine Brehaut, Blake Minton, Kirsty Rawlings and Fiona Tillet

Previously published as *Cooking with Honey*
Printed in Singapore

For all recipes, quantities are given in both metric and imperial measures and,
where appropriate, measures are also given in standard cups and spoons.
Follow one set, but not a mixture, because they are not interchangeable.

Contents

$\mathcal{I}$NTRODUCTION

Man's love affair with honey goes back thousands of years. Ancient rock paintings in southern Africa and Spain portray men harvesting wild honey, first by shinning unprotected up trees or rock-faces, and later using primitive ladders and smoking torches.

The earliest hives were probably accidental – the result of bees nesting in hollow trees, logs or pots – but honey hunters soon discovered that by trapping the queen in a container of their own making, woven perhaps from grass or reeds, they could have ready access to the delicious sweet treat.

The ancient Egyptians were proficient beekeepers, even moving their hives down the Nile, by donkey or boat, as the flowers that furnished the nectar came into bloom. They fed honey cakes to their sacred animals and used honey in many of their rituals, including the ceremonial burial of a pharaoh.

Honey has been used in healing and folk medicine for generations, continues to feature in face masks and other beauty products and is used to make soothing balms, but it is as a natural sweetener that it is most highly regarded. When the Aztecs found their chocolate a little too bitter, they simply stirred in a little honey. The ancient Greeks and Romans used it to make bread and cakes, and the French found honey the perfect sweetener for their famous *pain d'épices*. In Germany it surfaced in *lebkuchen*, while the Italians mixed it with nuts, cocoa, spices, candied peel and melon to make the popular

panforte. Today, honey is just as popular as an ingredient in savoury dishes, including salad dressings, casseroles, marinades and glazes for poultry and meat that is to be barbecued.

In Britain, beekeeping is an ancient tradition. The Druids called this land "The Isle of Honey" and mead was for centuries the national drink. Mead is still made today, and can be sweet or dry. Honey beer is a favourite is some parts of Africa. Unlike mead, it is made relatively rapidly and it is ready to drink 1–2 days after fermentation has begun. The original amber nectar also finds its way into a number of liqueurs, including Drambuie, which is made from Scotch whisky, herbs and honey scented with the fragrance of heather, and *Krupnik*, which is a Polish whisky and honey liqueur.

Whatever your favourite drink might be, raise a glass to honey and good health as you leaf through the pages of this book, planning another excellent meal based upon this exciting ingredient.

Jenny Fleetwood

Types of Honey

Orange Blossom
From the orange groves of Spain, Mexico, the USA, Israel and South Africa, this is a clear golden honey with a delicate citrus flavour. It is very good for cooking.

Acacia
This is a very light and delicate honey, ideal for sweetening hot or cold drinks. It tends to stay liquid in the jar, which makes it easy to mix into food or drinks.

Heather
With its subtle woody flavour, heather honey is extremely popular. Creamy in the jar, it liquefies when stirred, so is convenient to use.

Eucalyptus
Australia is the main source of this creamy honey. There are numerous native species of eucalyptus, so the appearance of the honey varies considerably, but the most commonly exported variety looks rather like peanut butter and has a distinctive toffee-like flavour.

English Set
Gathered from bees in England, set honey is honey which has been allowed to crystallize naturally.

Clover
North America's most popular honey, this is pale cream in colour. It has a smooth, mild flavour. Usually sold as a set honey, it is also available clear.

Honeycomb
This is a delicious treat, sold in some health food shops and speciality food stores. It is very fragile, and is therefore often sold in a miniature wooden frame. The entire comb is edible and is usually served in small squares.

Manuka
This monofloral honey (from a single source) comes from New Zealand. Dark and creamy, it is often packed in a dark amber pot to preserve the colour and aroma.

Cut Comb
This is also on sale in health shops and speciality shops. As the name suggests, this consists of bars sliced from a large honeycomb and wrapped separately.

Creamed floral and heather

English set

Cut comb honey

Acacia

Canadian clover

New Zealand manuka

Orange Blossom

Australian eucalyptus

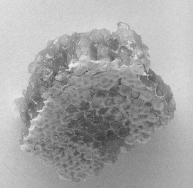

Honeycomb

$\mathcal{B}$ASIC $\mathcal{T}$ECHNIQUES

HONEY AND HEALTH

Ever since Athenaeus, a Greek writer and philosopher, asserted in the second century that those who ate honey every day for breakfast would be free from disease for the rest of their lives, extravagant claims have been made about honey. Although there is scant scientific evidence for most of these endorsements – honey is basically sugar – the belief in its medicinal qualities has persisted and is fundamental to folklore the world over.

• Honey is an easily assimilated source of unrefined sugars, and is a useful energy food for athletes.

• Honey is mildly antiseptic. It is used in some Eastern European countries for treating burns and wounds. Some germs cannot survive in honey.

• It is believed that honey is a natural sedative, and can be helpful in reducing stress levels.

• An English book on the properties of honey, published in the 18th century, recommended it for the treatment of asthma, coughs and hoarseness.

COOK'S TIPS

• For a simply delicious dessert, mix Greek-style yogurt with flaked almonds, then use a honey spoon to drizzle honey over the top.

• Honey is very good in salad dressings. Mix 15ml/1 tbsp clear honey with 150ml/¼ pint/⅔ cup white wine vinegar in a screw-top jar. Add plenty of salt and ground black pepper. Close the jar and shake well before using.

• To substitute honey for sugar in baking, use 175ml/6fl oz/ ¾ cup honey for every 225g/8oz/1 cup sugar specified. Use slightly less liquid and cook the cake or bread at a slightly lower temperature than the one suggested in the recipe.

• If you need to heat honey, do this very gently. High temperatures destroy the enzymes, may cause the sugar in the honey to caramelize and will almost certainly impair the flavour.

STORING AND USING HONEY

There is no difference, either nutritionally or chemically, between clear (liquid) honey and set honey. Most honey is syrupy when collected. Some types stay that way, but the majority soon start to granulate. What happens is that part of the glucose separates out as crystals. A network is rapidly established, so the honey looks solid. The crystals are pure white, so the honey gets lighter. The person marketing the honey decides whether it should be clear or set, bearing in mind the honey's natural properties and what the market requires. Americans tend to like their honey clear, but Canadians prefer the set type. Clear honey is heat-treated to discourage granulation; set honey is encouraged to form small evenly distributed crystals, so the honey is smooth, not grainy.

If clear honey granulates, simply place the jar in warm water. Use the same method to liquefy set honey.

It is not necessary – or even desirable – to store honey in the fridge. Keep it in a cool, dry place and it will last for a long time without loss of flavour.

HONEY AND HAZELNUT SPREAD

Try this superb spread on scones or hot toast.

Roast 75g/3oz/¾ cup hazelnuts, rub off the skins and grind the nuts in a food processor. Tip into a bowl and add 45ml/3 tbsp set honey and 30ml/ 2 tbsp double cream. Stir well until mixed then chill until the spread is set. Use the spread in 1–2 days. Makes about 250ml/8fl oz/1 cup.

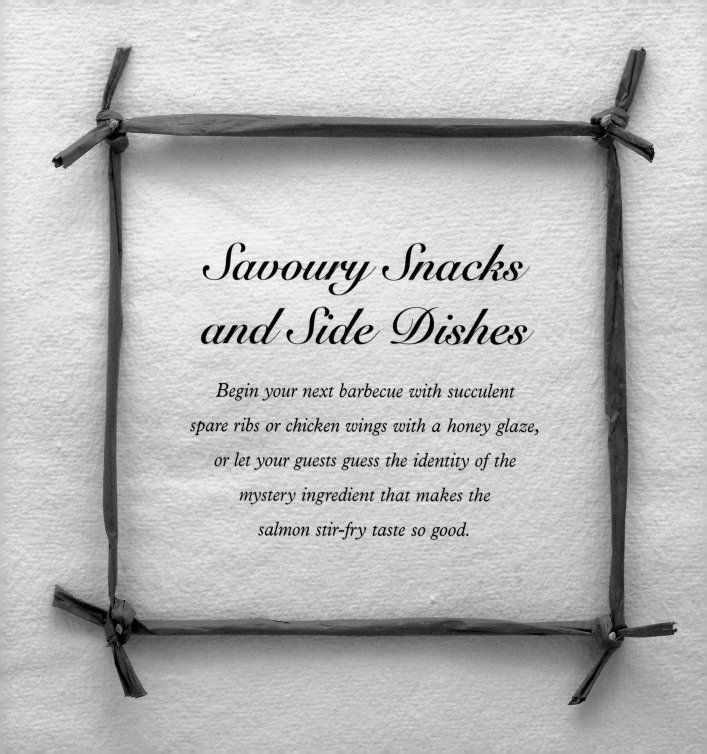

Savoury Snacks and Side Dishes

Begin your next barbecue with succulent
spare ribs or chicken wings with a honey glaze,
or let your guests guess the identity of the
mystery ingredient that makes the
salmon stir-fry taste so good.

HONEY-GLAZED SPARE RIBS

These delicious sticky ribs are easy to eat with fingers, once the little bones have been cleaned away at one end to provide handles.

Makes about 25

1kg/2¼lb meaty pork spare ribs, cut into 5cm/2in lengths
175ml/6fl oz/¾ cup tomato ketchup or mild chilli sauce
30–45ml/2–3 tbsp soy sauce
30–45ml/2–3 tbsp clear honey
2 garlic cloves, finely chopped
60ml/4 tbsp orange juice
1.5ml/¼ tsp cayenne pepper (or to taste)
1.5ml/¼ tsp Chinese five-spice powder
1–2 whole star anise

COOK'S TIP
Five-spice powder, made from ground cinnamon, star anise, cloves, ginger and fennel seeds, adds a delicious flavour to marinades, biscuits and pies.

Using a small sharp knife, scrape away about 5mm/¼in of meat from one end of each tiny spare rib, to serve as a little handle.

Mix the ketchup or chilli sauce, soy sauce, honey, garlic, orange juice, cayenne, five-spice powder and star anise in a large bowl or shallow baking dish until well blended. Add the ribs and toss to coat. Cover and chill for 6–8 hours or overnight.

Preheat the oven to 180°C/350°F/Gas 4. Line a baking sheet with foil and arrange the spare ribs in a single layer, spooning over any remaining marinade.

Bake uncovered, basting occasionally, for 1–1½ hours, or until the ribs are well browned and glazed. Serve warm or at room temperature.

HONEY CHOPS WITH GLAZED CARROTS

These tasty sticky chops are very quick and easy to prepare and grill. Serve them with herby mashed potatoes or chips.

Serves 4

4 pork loin chops
50g/2oz/¼ cup butter
30ml/2 tbsp clear honey
15ml/1 tbsp tomato purée

For the carrots

450g/1lb carrots
15g/½oz/1 tbsp butter
15ml/1 tbsp soft light brown sugar
15ml/1 tbsp sesame seeds, to serve

VARIATION
Use mustard instead of tomato purée, if you prefer. A whole grain mustard would be ideal.

Prepare the carrots: cut them into matchsticks, put them in a saucepan and add just enough cold water to cover. Stir in the butter and brown sugar and bring to the boil. Lower the heat and simmer for 15–20 minutes, until most of the liquid has boiled away. Preheat the grill to high.

Line the grill pan with foil and arrange the pork chops on the grill rack. Beat the butter and honey together and gradually beat in the tomato purée to make a smooth paste.

Spread half the honey paste over the chops and grill for 5 minutes, until browned. Turn the chops over, spread them with the remaining honey paste and grill the second side for 5 minutes, or until the meat is cooked through. Sprinkle the sesame seeds over the carrots and serve with the chops.

CHINESE HONEY-GLAZED CHICKEN WINGS

The honey makes these gloriously sticky, so make sure you provide finger bowls and paper napkins.

Serves 4

12 chicken wings

3 garlic cloves, crushed

4cm/1½in piece of fresh root
* ginger, grated*

juice of 1 large lemon

45ml/3 tbsp soy sauce

45ml/3 tbsp clear honey

2.5ml/½ tsp chilli powder

150ml/¼ pint/⅔ cup chicken stock

salt and ground black pepper

lemon wedges, to garnish

Remove the wing tips and cut each wing into two joints. Mix the garlic, ginger, lemon juice, soy sauce, honey, chilli powder and seasoning in a dish. Add the chicken pieces, turning to coat them. Cover with clear film and marinate overnight.

Preheat the oven to 220°C/425°F/Gas 7. Lift the wings out of the marinade and arrange them in a single layer in a roasting tin. Bake for 20–25 minutes, basting at least twice with the marinade during cooking.

Place the wings on a plate and keep them hot. Add the stock to the marinade in the roasting tin, and bring to the boil. Cook until syrupy, then spoon a little over the wings. Serve garnished with the lemon wedges.

COOK'S TIP

Use the wing tips from the pieces of chicken to make the stock, if you like. Add a slice each of carrot and onion, and a bay leaf.

Avocado Salad with Honey Dressing

This salad, with its delicate honey and mint dressing, makes an ideal starter for a summer dinner party.

Serves 6

1 pink grapefruit
1 yellow grapefruit
1 cantaloupe melon, halved
  and seeded
2 large, ripe but firm avocados
30ml/2 tbsp fresh lemon juice
30ml/2 tbsp vegetable oil
15ml/1 tbsp clear honey
45ml/3 tbsp chopped fresh mint
salt and ground black pepper
fresh mint leaves, to garnish

COOK'S TIP

If you do not have a melon baller, cut the melon into wedges, the same size as the grapefruit segments. Do the same with the avocados.

Peel and segment both grapefruit, using a sharp knife, and cut between the membranes. Put the segments in a bowl. With a melon baller, scoop out balls from the melon flesh and add them to the grapefruit. Chill the fruit for at least 30 minutes.

Cut the avocados in half and discard the stones. Peel off the skins, then cut the flesh into small pieces. Place in a bowl, add the lemon juice and toss to coat well. Using a slotted spoon, add the avocado to the grapefruit mixture. Reserve the remaining lemon juice.

Make the dressing by whisking the oil into the reserved lemon juice. Stir in the honey and chopped mint, with salt and pepper to taste. Pour the dressing over the fruit and toss gently. Garnish with mint leaves and serve.

PINEAPPLE, HONEY AND MINT CHUTNEY

This tasty fruit chutney goes particularly well with pork or lamb dishes.

Makes 750ml/1¼ pints/3 cups

250ml/8fl oz/1 cup raspberry vinegar

250ml/8fl oz/1 cup dry white wine

1 small pineapple, peeled
*   and chopped*

2 oranges, peeled and chopped

1 apple, peeled and chopped

1 red pepper, seeded and diced

2 small onions, finely chopped

50ml/2fl oz/¼ cup honey

pinch of salt

1 clove

4 black peppercorns

30ml/2 tbsp chopped fresh mint

In a saucepan, combine the vinegar and wine and bring to the boil. Boil for 3 minutes. Add the remaining ingredients, except the mint, and stir to blend. Simmer gently for about 30 minutes, stirring occasionally. Transfer to a strainer set over a bowl and drain, pressing down to extract the liquid. Remove and discard the clove and peppercorns. Set the fruit mixture aside.

Return the strained juice to the pan and boil until reduced by two-thirds. Pour over the fruit mixture.

Stir in the mint. Let the chutney stand for 6–8 hours before serving.

SPICED SALMON AND HONEY STIR-FRY

Marinating the salmon with honey allows all the flavours to develop, and the lime tenderizes the fish beautifully, so it needs very little stir-frying – be careful not to overcook it.

Serves 4

4 salmon steaks, about
*   225g/8oz each*
4 whole star anise
2 lemon grass stalks, sliced
juice of 3 limes
finely grated rind of 3 limes
30ml/2 tbsp clear honey
30ml/2 tbsp grapeseed oil
salt and ground black pepper
lime wedges, to garnish

COOK'S TIP

Sprinkle about 5ml/1 tsp salt on the cutting board before skinning the salmon and it will be much easier to handle and less likely to slide.

Remove the middle bone from each salmon steak to make two strips from each. Remove the skin and slice the salmon diagonally into pieces.

Roughly crush the star anise with a pestle in a mortar. Place in a non-metallic dish, with the lemon grass, lime juice and rind and honey. Mix well. Add the salmon, turning to coat the pieces in the mixture. Season well with salt and pepper, cover and chill overnight.

Lift the pieces of salmon out of the marinade and pat them dry on kitchen paper. Reserve the marinade.

Heat a wok, then add the oil. When the oil is hot, add the salmon and stir-fry, stirring constantly until cooked. Increase the heat, pour over the marinade and bring to the boil. Serve at once, garnished with the lime wedges.

HONEY-GLAZED CARROTS

Honey accentuates the natural sweetness of the carrots and orange juice adds a delicious piquancy.

Serves 6

*450g/1lb baby carrots, trimmed
  and peeled*

40g/1½oz butter or margarine

30ml/2 tbsp honey

30ml/2 tbsp fresh orange juice

*225g/8oz spring onions, cut
  diagonally into 2.5cm/1in lengths*

salt and ground black pepper

Cook the carrots in boiling salted water or steam them for 10 minutes until just tender. Drain if necessary.

In a frying pan, melt the butter or margarine with the honey and orange juice, stirring until the mixture is smooth and well combined.

Add the carrots and spring onions to the pan. Cook for about 5 minutes over a medium heat, stirring occasionally, until the vegetables are heated through and glazed. Season to taste before serving.

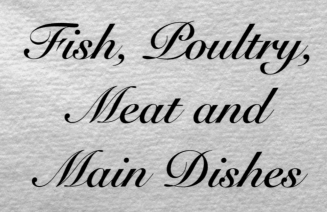

Fish, Poultry, Meat and Main Dishes

Although we tend to think of honey in terms of sweet dishes, it makes an admirable addition to all sorts of savouries, including roast gammon, panfried calf's liver and glazed poultry. Try the fruit and honey relish – it's perfect with pork.

HONEYED SALMON FILLETS

Honey, soy sauce and lime juice combine to make a marvellous marinade for grilled salmon.

Serves 6

900g/2lb salmon fillet, cut in 6 pieces

120ml/4fl oz/½ cup clear honey

60ml/4 tbsp soy sauce

juice of 2 limes

15ml/1 tbsp sesame oil

1.5ml/¼ tsp crushed dried chilli

1.5ml/¼ tsp crushed
   black peppercorns

lettuce, to garnish

COOK'S TIP

*The acid in the citrus juice
begins to "cook" the fish, so it
is only necessary to grill the
pieces on one side.*

Place the salmon pieces skin-side down in a baking dish large enough to hold them all in a single layer.

Combine the honey, soy sauce, lime juice, sesame oil, crushed chilli and peppercorns in a bowl. Mix well. Pour the mixture over the fish. Cover and marinate for 30 minutes.

Preheat the grill. Lift the fish out of the marinade and arrange on the rack in the grill pan, skin-side down. Grill about 7.5cm/3in from the heat for 6–8 minutes or until the fish flakes easily. Garnish with lettuce and serve.

HONEY-ROAST CHICKEN

A honey glaze not only gives roast chicken a glorious golden skin – it also improves the flavour.

Serves 4

1 chicken, about 1.5kg/3–3½lb
30ml/2 tbsp clear honey
15ml/1 tbsp brandy
25ml/1½ tbsp plain flour
150ml/¼ pint/⅔ cup chicken stock
green beans, to serve

For the stuffing

4 rindless bacon rashers, chopped
2 shallots, chopped
50g/2oz/¾ cup button
*   mushrooms, quartered*
15g/½oz/1 tbsp butter or margarine
2 thick slices of white bread, diced
15ml/1 tbsp chopped fresh parsley
salt and ground black pepper

> COOK'S TIP
> *Use smoked streaky bacon for*
> *the stuffing.*

Make the stuffing. Heat the bacon in a frying pan until the fat runs, then add the shallots and mushrooms and fry over a medium heat for 5 minutes. With a slotted spoon, transfer the bacon and vegetables to a bowl.

Pour off all but 30ml/2 tbsp bacon fat from the pan. Add the butter or margarine. When it is hot, fry the diced bread until golden brown. Add it to the bacon mixture, stir in the parsley and add salt and pepper to taste. Allow to cool. Preheat the oven to 180°C/350°F/Gas 4.

Pack the stuffing into the body cavity of the chicken. Truss it neatly, then place it in a roasting tin.

Mix the honey with the brandy. Brush half the mixture over the chicken. Roast for 1¼–1½ hours, until the chicken is thoroughly cooked. Baste the chicken frequently with the remaining honey mixture during roasting.

Transfer the chicken to a warmed serving platter. Cover with foil and set aside. Strain the cooking juices into a jug. Skim off the surface fat.

Stir the flour into the sediment in the roasting tin. Add the remaining degreased cooking juices and the stock. Boil rapidly until the gravy has thickened, stirring constantly. Pour the gravy into a warmed sauceboat and serve with the chicken and lightly cooked green beans.

HONEY AND ORANGE-GLAZED CHICKEN

Try orange-blossom honey for this tasty glaze. It makes a perfect partner for chicken and oranges.

Serve 4

4 chicken breasts, about 175g/6oz
    each, boned and skinned
15ml/1 tbsp oil
4 spring onions, chopped
1 garlic clove, crushed
45ml/3 tbsp clear honey
60ml/4 tbsp fresh orange juice
1 orange, peeled and segmented
30ml/2 tbsp soy sauce
fresh lemon balm or flat leaf parsley
    sprigs, to garnish
baked potatoes and salad, to serve

VARIATION
*The sauce is equally good when
served with pork steaks.*

Preheat the oven to 190°C/375°F/Gas 5. Place the chicken breasts in a shallow roasting tin and set aside.

Heat the oil in a small pan. Fry the spring onions and crushed garlic for 2 minutes until softened. Add the honey, orange juice, orange segments and soy sauce to the pan, stirring well until the honey has dissolved.

Pour the mixture over the chicken and bake, uncovered, for 45 minutes, basting once or twice, until the chicken is cooked through. Serve on plates, garnished with lemon balm or parsley, accompanied by baked potatoes and a fresh salad.

HONEY-COATED DUCK

Crisp honey-glazed duck in a mandarin sauce, served with stir-fried vegetables, makes a tasty dish.

Serves 4

4 duck legs or boneless breasts

30ml/2 tbsp light soy sauce

45ml/3 tbsp clear honey

15ml/1 tbsp sesame seeds

4 mandarin oranges

5ml/1 tsp cornflour

salt and ground black pepper

COOK'S TIP

Pricking the duck skin all over allows much of the fat to drain away, but the meat remains marvellously moist.

Preheat the oven to 180°C/350°F/Gas 4. Prick the duck skin all over with a fork. If using breasts of duck, slash the skin diagonally at intervals with a sharp knife.

Place the duck joints on a rack in a roasting tin and roast for 1 hour. Meanwhile, mix 15ml/1 tbsp of the soy sauce with 30ml/2 tbsp of the honey. Remove the duck from the oven, brush with the honey mixture and sprinkle with the sesame seeds. Roast for 15–20 minutes more, until golden brown.

Grate the rind from 1 mandarin and squeeze the juice from 2 of them. Mix the rind and juice in a small pan. Stir in the cornflour, then the remaining soy sauce and honey. Heat, stirring, until the sauce thickens and clears. Add salt and pepper to taste, and keep hot. Peel and slice the remaining mandarins. Serve the duck with the mandarin slices and the sauce.

PORK WITH FRUIT AND HONEY RELISH

Roasted chilli, nectarines and honey make a harmonious mixture to serve with grilled pork chops.

Serves 4

250ml/8fl oz/1 cup fresh orange juice

45ml/3 tbsp olive oil

2 garlic cloves, crushed

5ml/1 tsp ground cumin

15ml/1 tbsp coarsely ground
    black pepper

8 pork loin chops, about 2cm/¾in
    thick, well trimmed

salt

nectarine slices, lettuce and chervil
    sprigs, to garnish

For the relish

1 small fresh green chilli

30ml/2 tbsp clear honey

juice of ½ lemon

250ml/8fl oz/1 cup chicken stock

2 nectarines, stoned and chopped

1 garlic clove, crushed

½ onion, finely chopped

5ml/1 tsp finely chopped fresh
    root ginger

1.5ml/¼ tsp salt

15ml/1 tbsp chopped fresh coriander

Make the relish. Roast the chilli over a gas flame, holding it with tongs, until charred on all sides. (Alternatively, char the skin under the grill.) Set aside to cool for 5 minutes. Carefully rub off the charred skin from the chilli. Chop the chilli finely, discarding the seeds if you prefer a milder flavour, and put it in a saucepan. Add all the remaining ingredients except the coriander. Bring to the boil, then lower the heat and simmer, stirring occasionally, for about 30 minutes. Stir in the coriander and set aside.

In a small bowl, combine the orange juice, oil, garlic, cumin and pepper. Stir to mix. Arrange the pork chops in a shallow dish large enough to hold them all in a single layer. Pour over the orange juice mixture and turn to coat. Cover and leave to stand for at least 1 hour, or refrigerate overnight.

Lift the pork chops out of the marinade and pat them dry with kitchen paper.

Heat a ridged grill pan. When hot, add the pork chops and cook for 5 minutes, until browned. Turn and cook the other side for 10 minutes or more, until cooked through. Serve at once, with the relish. Garnish with nectarine slices, lettuce and chervil.

HONEY-ROAST GAMMON

A honey-glazed gammon joint makes the perfect centrepiece for a celebration meal, whether you serve it hot or cold. Cumberland sauce is the perfect accompaniment.

Serves 8–10

1 boned middle gammon joint, about
  2kg/4½lb
1 onion, quartered
cloves
2 bay leaves
few black peppercorns
pared rind of ½ orange
small piece of fresh root ginger
½ cinnamon stick
few parsley stalks
cranberry jelly, apple sauce or
  Cumberland sauce, to serve

For the glaze

cloves
90ml/6 tbsp clear honey
30ml/2 tbsp whole grain mustard

Weigh the gammon and calculate the cooking time at 20 minutes per 450g/1lb, plus 20 minutes extra. Place the gammon in a large pan and cover with cold water. Bring to the boil and remove from the heat. Pour off the water, rinse the pan and replace the joint. Cover it with cold water and add the onion quarters, studded with cloves, and the bay leaves, peppercorns, orange rind, ginger, cinnamon and parsley stalks. Bring slowly to the boil, cover the pan and lower the heat. Simmer for the calculated cooking time less 15 minutes. In the case of a gammon weighing 2kg/4½lb, this would be 1 hour 35 minutes.

Lift the gammon out of the pan (reserve the stock for soups, casseroles and sauces) and allow it to cool slightly. Cut off the rind from the ham as evenly as possible and score the fat in a diamond pattern with a sharp knife. Preheat the oven to 180°C/350°F/Gas 4.

Press cloves into the scored gammon fat at intervals. Mix the honey and mustard in a bowl and spread it over the skin. Wrap the gammon in foil, leaving only the glazed area uncovered.

Place the gammon, glazed-side up, in a roasting tin and bake for about 15 minutes. Serve hot or cold, with cranberry jelly, apple sauce or its traditional accompaniment, Cumberland sauce.

SAUTEED LIVER WITH HONEY

A wonderful sweet-and-sour sauce, made from honey and sherry vinegar, proves the perfect foil for tender calves' liver in this recipe from France.

Serves 4

4 slices of calves' liver, about
  175g/6oz each
plain flour, for dusting
25g/1oz/2 tbsp butter
30ml/2 tbsp vegetable oil
30ml/2 tbsp sherry vinegar or red
  wine vinegar
30–45ml/2–3 tbsp chicken stock
15ml/1 tbsp clear honey
salt and ground black pepper
watercress sprigs, to garnish

COOK'S TIP
The calves' liver should be cut about 1cm/½in thick. Cook it until it is well browned on the outside but still slightly pink in the centre.

Wipe the liver slices with damp kitchen paper, then season both sides with a little salt and pepper and dust the slices lightly with flour, shaking off any excess.

In a large heavy frying pan, melt half of the butter with the oil over a high heat and swirl to blend.

Add the liver slices to the pan and cook for 1–2 minutes until browned on one side, then turn and cook for 1 minute more. Transfer to heated plates and keep hot.

Stir the vinegar, stock and honey into the pan. Boil for 1 minute, stirring constantly, then add the remaining butter, stirring until melted and smooth. Spoon over the liver slices, garnish with watercress sprigs and serve.

HONEY-GLAZED LAMB

Lemon and honey is a classic combination, perfect for both savoury and sweet dishes.

Serves 4

450g/1lb boneless lean lamb

15ml/1 tbsp grapeseed oil

175g/6oz mangetouts, trimmed

3 spring onions, sliced

30ml/2 tbsp clear honey

juice of ½ lemon

30ml/2 tbsp chopped fresh coriander

15ml/1 tbsp sesame seeds

salt and ground black pepper

coriander sprigs, to garnish

lemon slices, to serve

COOK'S TIP

Use stir-fry oil for frying, if you like. A blend of sunflower oil and sesame oil is full of flavour and does not readily burn at high temperatures.

Using a sharp knife, cut the lamb into thin strips. Heat a wok, then add the oil. When the oil is hot, stir-fry the lamb until browned all over. Remove from the wok with a slotted spoon and keep hot.

Add the mangetouts and spring onions to the oil remaining in the hot wok and stir-fry for 30 seconds.

Return the lamb to the wok and add the honey, lemon juice, coriander and sesame seeds, with plenty of salt and pepper. Bring to the boil and bubble for 1 minute until the lamb is well coated in the honey mixture. Serve at once with lemon slices and garnished with coriander sprigs.

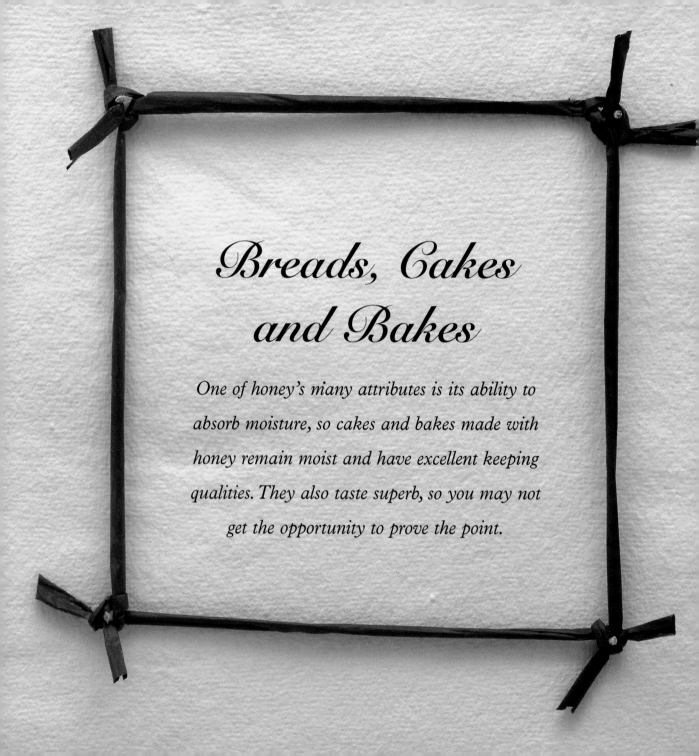

Breads, Cakes and Bakes

One of honey's many attributes is its ability to absorb moisture, so cakes and bakes made with honey remain moist and have excellent keeping qualities. They also taste superb, so you may not get the opportunity to prove the point.

WALNUT AND HONEY BREAD

Honey gives this nutty bread a superb flavour that intensifies the longer you keep it.

Makes 1 loaf

275g/10oz/2½ cups wholemeal flour
115g/4oz/1 cup strong white flour
10ml/2 tsp salt
10g/¼oz sachet easy-blend
  dried yeast
30ml/2 tbsp clear honey
475ml/16fl oz/2 cups hand-hot water
150g/5oz/1¼ cups walnut pieces,
  plus extra to decorate
1 beaten egg, to glaze

COOK'S TIP

Flours vary in their
absorbency, so you may need to
add a little more water when
making the dough.

Combine the flours, salt and yeast in a bowl. Make a well in the centre. Dissolve the honey in the water, then pour the mixture into the well and stir to obtain a smooth dough. Add more flour if the dough is too sticky and use your hands if the dough becomes too stiff to stir. Knead the dough, adding flour if necessary, until smooth and elastic. Knead in the walnuts.

Shape the walnut and honey dough into a round loaf and place it on a greased baking sheet. Press in more walnut pieces to decorate the top. Cover loosely and leave to rise in a warm place until doubled in size.

Preheat the oven to 220°C/425°F/Gas 7. Score the top of the loaf with a sharp knife. Brush with the egg. Bake for 15 minutes, then lower the oven temperature to 190°C/375°F/Gas 5 and bake for 40 minutes, or until the bottom of the loaf sounds hollow when tapped. Cool on a wire rack.

HONEY GRAIN BREAD

This is a particularly tasty loaf, with a subtle hint of honey. Serve toasted, spread with butter and honey.

Makes 2 loaves

65g/2½oz/generous ¾ cup rolled oats
600ml/1 pint/2½ cups milk
60ml/4 tbsp sunflower oil
50g/2oz/⅓ cup soft light brown sugar
30ml/2 tbsp clear honey
450g/1lb/4 cups strong white flour
175g/6oz/2 cups soya flour
350g/12oz/3 cups wholemeal flour
25g/1oz/½ cup wheatgerm
10ml/2 tsp salt
2 x 10g/¼oz sachets easy-blend
  dried yeast
2 eggs, lightly beaten

COOK'S TIP

To test the loaves, hold each upside down in an oven-gloved hand. Make a fist of your other hand and tap gently on the bottom of the loaf. If it sounds hollow, the loaf is done.

Put the oats in a large bowl. Heat the milk in a saucepan until just below boiling point, then pour it over the oats. Stir in the oil, sugar and honey. Cool the mixture to hand-hot.

Combine the flours, wheatgerm, salt and yeast in a large mixing bowl. Add the oat mixture and eggs and mix to a rough dough. Knead on a lightly floured surface for about 10 minutes, until smooth and elastic.

Grease two 23 x 13cm/9 x 5in loaf tins. Divide the dough into four equal pieces and roll each to a rope slightly longer than the tin and about 4cm/1½in thick. Twist the ropes together in pairs and place in the tins. Cover loosely and leave to rise in a warm place until doubled in size.

Preheat the oven to 220°C/425°F/Gas 7. Bake the honey loaves for 30–35 minutes, then remove from the tins and cool on a wire rack.

Yogurt Honey Muffins

There's quite a lot of honey in these muffins, so choose a light subtle-flavoured variety such as acacia.

Makes 12

50g/2oz/4 tbsp butter
75ml/5 tbsp clear honey
250ml/8fl oz/1 cup natural yogurt
1 size 2 egg
grated rind of 1 lemon
60ml/4 tbsp fresh lemon juice
115g/4oz/1 cup plain flour
115g/4oz/1 cup wholemeal flour
7.5ml/1½ tsp bicarbonate of soda
pinch of grated nutmeg

VARIATION

For a more substantial muffin,
fold in 50g/2oz/½ cup chopped
walnuts with the flour.

Preheat the oven to 190°C/375°F/Gas 5. Grease a 12-cup muffin tin or use paper liners. Melt the butter with the honey in a saucepan. Remove from the heat and set aside to cool slightly.

In a bowl, whisk together the yogurt, egg, lemon rind and juice. Add the butter and honey mixture. Mix well.

Sift the dry ingredients into a second bowl, then fold them into the yogurt mixture until just blended.

Fill the prepared muffin cups two-thirds full. Bake for 20–25 minutes, or until the tops spring back when lightly touched. Leave to cool in the tin for 5 minutes before turning the muffins out on to a wire rack. Serve warm or at room temperature.

ORANGE HONEY BREAD

Honey improves the keeping quality of cakes and breads, but this is so delicious that you are unlikely to be able to put the theory to the test.

Makes 1 loaf

275g/10oz/2½ cups plain flour

12.5ml/2½ tsp baking powder

2.5ml/½ tsp bicarbonate of soda

2.5ml/½ tsp salt

25g/1oz/2 tbsp margarine

250ml/8fl oz/1 cup clear honey

1 egg, lightly beaten

20ml/4 tbsp grated orange rind

175ml/6fl oz/¾ cup fresh
  orange juice

75g/3oz/¾ cup chopped walnuts

Preheat the oven to 160°C/325°F/Gas 3. Grease a 23 x 13cm/9 x 5in loaf tin and line the base with non-stick baking paper. Sift the flour, baking powder, bicarbonate of soda and salt together.

Cream the margarine in a mixing bowl until soft. Stir in the honey until well mixed, then stir in the lightly beaten egg. Add the orange rind and stir to combine thoroughly.

Fold the flour mixture into the honey and egg mixture in three batches, alternating with the orange juice. Stir in the walnuts.

Pour into the prepared tin and bake for about 1 hour, or until a cake tester inserted in the centre of the loaf comes out clean. Leave to stand for 10 minutes before turning out on to a wire rack to cool.

BANANA AND HONEY LOAF

For the best flavour and a really good, moist texture, use very ripe bananas for this cake.

Makes 1 loaf

75g/3oz/²⁄₃ cup wholemeal flour

75g/3oz/²⁄₃ cup plain flour

5ml/1 tsp baking powder

5ml/1 tsp ground mixed spice

45ml/3 tbsp chopped
*   hazelnuts, toasted*

2 large ripe bananas

1 egg

30ml/2 tbsp sunflower oil, plus extra
*   for greasing*

30ml/2 tbsp clear honey

grated rind and juice of 1 orange

4 orange slices, halved, and 5ml/1 tsp
*   icing sugar, to decorate*

COOK'S TIP

If you plan to keep the loaf for more than three days, omit the orange slices. Instead, brush with honey and sprinkle with slivered hazelnuts.

Preheat the oven to 180°C/350°F/Gas 4. Brush a 23 x 13cm/9 x 5in loaf tin lightly with oil and line the base with non-stick baking paper.

Sift the flours with the baking powder and spice into a large bowl, adding any bran that remains in the sieve. Stir in the hazelnuts.

Mash the bananas in a mixing bowl. Beat in the egg, oil, honey, orange rind and juice. Add to the dry ingredients and mix well.

Spoon the mixture into the prepared tin and smooth the surface. Bake for 40–45 minutes, or until firm and golden brown. Turn out on to a wire rack to cool. Preheat the grill.

Sprinkle the orange slices with the icing sugar and grill until golden. Cool slightly, then use to decorate the loaf.

HONEY-GLAZED APPLE PIE

Here's your chance to experiment with a honey flavour that you feel best suits your chosen apples. Try a heather honey, perhaps, or a Jamaican tropical flower variety.

Serves 8

275g/10oz/2½ cups plain flour

2.5ml/½ tsp salt

115g/4oz/½ cup chilled unsalted butter, diced

50g/2oz/¼ cup chilled vegetable fat, diced

75–90ml/5–6 tbsp iced water

1.5kg/3–3½lb firm eating or cooking apples, peeled, cored and sliced

50g/2oz/¼ cup sugar

10ml/2 tsp ground cinnamon

grated rind and juice of 1 lemon

25g/1oz/2 tbsp butter for the apples, diced

30–45ml/2–3 tbsp clear honey, melted

Sift the flour and salt into a bowl. Rub in the fats until the mixture resembles coarse breadcrumbs. Stir in enough iced water to moisten the dry ingredients, then gather together to make a ball. Wrap the pastry and chill for 30 minutes. Preheat the oven to 200°C/400°F/Gas 6.

Put the apple slices, sugar, cinnamon, lemon rind and juice in a bowl and toss together well.

Roll out the pastry to a 30cm/12in round. Fit the pastry in the pie dish so that the excess dough overhangs the edges. Fill with the apple mixture, then fold in the edges, crimping them loosely to make a decorative border. Dot the apples with the diced butter.

Bake the pie for 45 minutes, until the pastry is golden and the apples tender. Remove from the oven and brush the honey over the apples to glaze.

PECAN AND HONEY BARS

Honey and nuts go very well together, as this American recipe proves. If you can't find pecan nuts, use walnuts instead.

Makes 36 squares
225g/8oz/2 cups plain flour
pinch of salt
115g/4oz/½ cup granulated sugar
225g/8oz/1 cup butter or
  margarine, diced
1 egg
finely grated rind of 1 lemon

For the topping
175g/6oz/¾ cup butter
50ml/2fl oz/¼ cup clear honey
60ml/4 tbsp granulated sugar
175g/6oz/¾ cup soft dark
  brown sugar
75ml/5 tbsp whipping cream
450g/1lb/4 cups pecan nuts

Lightly grease a 35 x 28cm/14 x 11in Swiss roll tin. Sift the flour and salt into a bowl. Stir in the sugar, then rub in the fat until the mixture resembles coarse breadcrumbs. Blend in the egg and lemon rind.

Press the mixture into the prepared tin and prick the pastry all over with a fork. Chill for 10 minutes. Preheat the oven to 190°C/375°F/Gas 5.

Bake the pastry for 15 minutes, then remove the tin from the oven (leave the oven on). Heat the butter, honey and sugars in a pan until melted, then bring to the boil and boil without stirring for 2 minutes. Remove from the heat and stir in the cream and pecan nuts. Pour over the base, return the tin to the oven and bake for 25 minutes. Cool in the tin.

Run a knife around the pastry edge, invert on to a baking sheet, place another sheet on top and invert again. Cut into squares for serving.

BAKLAVA

In Greece, the wonderful herb honey from Mount Hymettus would be used for this sweet filo pastry. Dark, clear and slightly thick, it owes its flavour to thyme and marjoram blossoms.

Makes 10 pieces

75g/3oz/6 tbsp butter, melted

6 large sheets of filo pastry

*225g/8oz/2 cups chopped mixed nuts
(such as almonds, pistachios,
hazelnuts and walnuts)*

50g/2oz/1 cup fresh breadcrumbs

5ml/1 tsp ground cinnamon

5ml/1 tsp mixed spice

2.5ml/½ tsp grated nutmeg

250ml/8fl oz/1 cup clear honey

60ml/4 tbsp lemon juice

Preheat the oven to 180°C/350°F/Gas 4. Butter a 28 x 18cm/11 x 7in tin. Unroll the filo pastry, brush one sheet with melted butter and use it to line the tin, easing it carefully up the sides. Repeat the process with two more sheets of filo, easing the pastry into the corners and letting the edges overhang the tin.

Mix the nuts, breadcrumbs and spices in a bowl and spoon this mixture evenly into the lined tin.

Cut the remaining three sheets of filo pastry in half widthways and brush each one with a little of the butter. Layer half the pieces of filo on top of the filling and fold in any overhanging edges. Top with the remaining buttered filo. With a sharp knife, mark the baklava diagonally into diamonds. Bake for about 30 minutes, until the pastry is golden.

Meanwhile, heat the honey and lemon juice gently in a pan. When the baklava is cooked, remove it from the oven and pour the syrup over while still warm. Leave to cool completely, then cut into diamonds, following the markings in the pastry, and serve.

COOK'S TIP

Filo pastry dries out very quickly, so keep any pieces not being used covered with a lightly dampened dish towel.

GREEK HONEY AND LEMON CAKE

To be authentic, you should use a Greek blossom honey, such as Hymettus, for this cake, but clear clover honey would also be good.

Makes 16 slices

40g/1½oz/3 tbsp butter or margarine
60ml/4 tbsp clear honey
finely grated rind and juice of
  1 lemon
150ml/¼ pint/⅔ cup milk
150g/5oz/1¼ cups plain flour
7.5ml/1½ tsp baking powder
2.5ml/½ tsp grated nutmeg
40g/1½oz/¼ cup semolina
2 egg whites
5ml/2 tsp sesame seeds

COOK'S TIP

Use a clean metal spoon and a figure-of-eight action when you fold the egg whites into the cake mixture.

Preheat the oven to 200°C/400°F/Gas 6. Grease a 19cm/7½in square deep cake tin and line the base with non-stick baking paper. Mix the butter or margarine with 45ml/3 tbsp of the honey in a saucepan and heat gently until melted. Reserve 15ml/1 tbsp lemon juice. Stir the rest into the honey mixture, with the lemon rind and milk.

Sift the flour, baking powder and nutmeg into a bowl, then beat in the honey mixture with the semolina. Whisk the egg whites until they form soft peaks, then fold them evenly into the mixture.

Spoon the mixture into the tin and sprinkle with sesame seeds. Bake for 25–30 minutes, until golden brown. Mix the reserved honey and lemon juice and drizzle over the cake while warm. Cool in the tin, then cut into fingers.

HONEY APPLE CAKE

Honey makes this a moist cutting cake. Instead of using apples, try making it with pears for a change.

Serves 8

115g/4oz/½ cup butter or margarine

175ml/6fl oz/¾ cup clear honey

3 eggs, beaten

175g/6oz/1½ cups plain flour

175g/6oz/1½ cups wholemeal flour

2.5ml/½ tsp salt

2.5ml/½ tsp bicarbonate of soda

few drops of vanilla essence

1 large eating apple

45–60ml/3–4 tbsp milk or apple juice

few apple slices and 15–30ml/2–3 tbsp

*   demerara sugar, for topping*

butter, to serve (optional)

COOK'S TIP

Substituting honey for some or all of the sugar in a creamed cake mixture like this one gives a delicious flavour.

Preheat the oven to 180°C/350°F/Gas 4. Grease an 18cm/7in square or 20cm/8in round cake tin. Cream the butter and honey until soft and pale. Beat in the eggs, then fold in the dry ingredients and vanilla essence.

Peel, core and grate the apple. Stir it into the mixture, with enough of the milk or apple juice to give a soft dropping consistency. Spoon the mixture into the tin and smooth the surface.

Bake for 30 minutes, then arrange the apple slices on the top and sprinkle generously with demerara sugar. Continue cooking for 30 minutes more, or until the cake is just firm to the touch.

Turn off the heat and leave the cake to cool in the oven. Remove from the tin before it is completely cold and wrap in foil to store. Serve sliced, with butter or simply on its own.

Cold Desserts

*Some of the simplest and most delicious desserts
are based on honey. Whether your fancy is for
fresh fruit with a honey dip, a creamy ice or a
wonderful whisky-flavoured whip, honey ensures
the sweet taste of success.*

HONEY AND MANGO CHEESECAKE

Use a fragrant citrus honey to complement the mango and lime in this exotic cheesecake.

Serves 4

40g/1½oz/3 tbsp butter or
margarine, softened
30ml/2 tbsp clear honey
225g/8oz/2 cups oatmeal
1 large ripe mango, peeled, stoned
and roughly chopped
275g/10oz/1¼ cups cream cheese
175ml/6fl oz/¾ cup natural yogurt
finely grated rind of 1 small lime
45ml/3 tbsp apple juice
20ml/4 tsp powdered gelatine
fresh mango and lime slices, to
decorate

VARIATION

Use drained canned mango
slices instead of fresh, if you
prefer, but add a few drops of
fresh lime juice to counteract
the sweetness.

Preheat the oven to 200°C/400°F/Gas 6. Cream the butter or margarine with the honey in a bowl, then stir in the oatmeal. Press the mixture into the base of a 20cm/8in loose-bottomed cake tin. Bake for 12–15 minutes, until lightly browned. Cool.

Place the chopped mango, cheese, yogurt and lime rind in a food processor or blender and process until smooth.

Put the apple juice in a small heatproof bowl and sprinkle the gelatine on top. When spongy, set over simmering water and stir until the gelatine has dissolved. Stir into the cheese mixture.

Pour the filling over the cheesecake base and chill until set, then remove from the tin and place on a serving plate. Decorate the top with the mango and lime slices.

VANILLA AND HONEY ICE CREAM

Honey ice cream is delicious. Pour a little Drambuie or other whisky and honey liqueur over the top for an extra-special treat.

Serves 4
250ml/8fl oz/1 cup buttermilk
60ml/4 tbsp double cream
1 vanilla pod or 2.5ml/ $\frac{1}{2}$ tsp
   vanilla essence
2 eggs
30ml/2 tbsp clear honey

VARIATION
Ice cream can be used as a base for other flavours: stir in puréed or chopped fruit, dissolved instant coffee or citrus rind, or coat the frozen roll in a layer of desiccated coconut or chopped nuts.

Place the buttermilk and cream in a pan. At this point, add the vanilla pod, if using, and heat gently until the mixture is almost boiling. Remove the pod. Put the eggs in a heatproof bowl. Place over a pan of hot water and whisk until pale and thick. Pour in the heated buttermilk mixture in a thin stream, whisking constantly. Continue whisking over the hot water until the mixture thickens slightly.

Whisk in the honey and if using vanilla essence, add at this point. Spoon the mixture into a freezer tub and freeze until the mixture is firm enough to hold its shape, then spoon it on to a sheet of non-stick baking paper. Form the semi-frozen ice cream into a sausage shape and roll it up in the paper. Freeze again until firm. Slice the ice cream, giving it a few minutes to soften before serving.

BANANA-HONEY YOGURT ICE

Invented for slimmers, this honey ice is a winner with everyone.

Serves 4–6

4 ripe bananas, roughly chopped

15ml/1 tbsp lemon juice

30ml/2 tbsp clear honey

250ml/8fl oz/1 cup thick
*   natural yogurt*

2.5ml/½ tsp ground cinnamon

dessert biscuits, slivered hazelnuts,
*   and banana slices, to serve*

Mix the bananas, lemon juice, honey, yogurt and cinnamon in a food processor or blender. Process until smooth and creamy. Pour into a freezer container and freeze until almost solid. Spoon back into the food processor or blender and process again until smooth.

Return the mixture to the tub and freeze again until firm. Allow to soften at room temperature for 15 minutes, then serve in scoops with dessert biscuits, slivered hazelnuts and banana slices.

49

Strawberry and Honey Pashka

This version of a traditional Russian dessert of cream cheese flavoured with honey is ideal for dinner parties – make it a day or two in advance for best results.

Serves 4

350g/12oz/1½ cups cottage cheese or
*   cream cheese*
175ml/6fl oz/¾ cup natural yogurt
30ml/2 tbsp clear honey
2.5ml/½ tsp rosewater
450g/1lb/2½ cups strawberries
handful of scented pink rose petals, to
*   decorate*

If using cottage cheese, drain off any liquid and pour the cheese into a sieve. Use a wooden spoon to rub it through the sieve into a mixing bowl. If using cream cheese, simply beat it lightly to soften. Stir in the yogurt, honey and rosewater.

Chop about half the strawberries and stir them into the cheese mixture.

Line a new, clean flowerpot or a sieve with fine cheesecloth and tip the cheese mixture into it. Leave it to drain over a mixing bowl for several hours, or overnight.

Invert the flowerpot or sieve on to a serving plate, turn out the pashka and remove the cheesecloth. Slice the reserved strawberries in half, leaving the greenery in place, and use with the rose petals to decorate the pashka.

Cook's Tip

A flowerpot shape is traditional for pashka, but you could make it in any shape – the small porcelain heart-shape moulds with draining holes used for coeurs à la crème *make a pretty alternative.*

ORANGE, HONEY AND MINT TERRINE

Orange blossom honey is the best choice for this refreshing dessert. It is ideal for serving after a rich meal as it is a good palate cleanser.

Serves 6

8–10 oranges

600ml/1 pint/2½ cups fresh
   orange juice

30ml/2 tbsp clear honey

20ml/4 tsp agar-agar

45ml/3 tbsp fresh mint, chopped

mint leaves, to decorate (optional)

COOK'S TIP

Agar-agar is the vegetarian's preferred setting agent as it comes from a non-meat source. If you prefer, use 1 sachet of powdered gelatine, softened in 30ml/2 tbsp cold water.

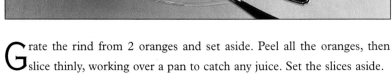

Grate the rind from 2 oranges and set aside. Peel all the oranges, then slice thinly, working over a pan to catch any juice. Set the slices aside.

Add the measured orange juice to the orange juice in the pan, with the honey, reserved rind and agar-agar. Stir the mixture over a gentle heat until the honey and agar-agar have dissolved.

Pack the orange slices into a 1kg/2¼lb loaf tin, sprinkling the mint between the layers. Slowly pour over the hot orange juice. Tap the tin lightly so that all the juice settles. Chill the terrine for several hours or overnight, until it is quite firm. When ready to serve, dip the tin briefly into very hot water and turn the terrine out on to a wet platter. Decorate with more mint leaves, if you like. Serve cut into thick slices.

GINGER AND HONEY WINTER FRUITS

A compote of dried fruit flavoured with honey is equally tasty as a dessert or breakfast dish. Serve it with lashings of Greek yogurt or cream.

Serves 4

1 lemon

4 green cardamom pods

1 cinnamon stick

150ml/¼ pint/⅔ cup clear honey

30ml/2 tbsp ginger syrup, from the jar

450g/1lb/2½ cups dried fruit salad

3 pieces of stem ginger

1 orange, peeled and segmented

Thinly pare 2 strips of rind from the lemon. Lightly crush the cardamom pods with the back of a heavy-bladed knife. Place the lemon rind, cardamoms, cinnamon stick, honey and ginger syrup in a heavy-based saucepan. Pour in 60ml/4 tbsp water and add the dried fruit. Bring to the boil, then lower the heat and simmer for 10 minutes. Pour into a serving bowl. Set aside until cool.

Chop the ginger and stir it into the fruit salad, with the orange segments. Cover and chill until ready to serve.

VARIATION
Omit the ginger syrup and use 30ml/2 tbsp rosewater instead. Add 50g/2oz/½ cup blanched almonds as well.

GRAPE AND HONEY WHIP

Frosted grapes add the finishing touches to this simple dessert, which is sweetened with clear honey.

Serves 4

115g/4oz/1 cup black or green
* seedless grapes, plus 4 sprigs*
2 egg whites
15ml/1 tbsp granulated sugar
finely grated rind and juice of
* ½ lemon*
250g/9oz/1 cup cream cheese
45ml/3 tbsp clear honey
30ml/2 tbsp brandy (optional)

VARIATION
Instead of brandy, use a honey-based liqueur such as Irish Mist, made from Irish whiskey, heather honey and herbs.

Brush the sprigs of grapes lightly with some of the egg whites and sprinkle with sugar to coat. Leave to dry.

Pour the lemon juice into a bowl and stir in the rind, cheese, honey and brandy, if using. Chop the remaining grapes and stir them in.

Whisk the remaining egg whites until they are stiff enough to hold soft peaks. Fold them into the grape mixture, then spoon into serving glasses. Top with the sugar-frosted grapes and serve chilled.

FRUDITÉS WITH HONEY DIP

Some of the simplest desserts are also the most delectable. This takes only minutes to make but tastes absolutely wonderful, making use of the classic honey and yogurt combination.

Serves 4

*250ml/8fl oz/1 cup thick natural
   yogurt
45ml/3 tbsp clear honey
selection of fresh fruit for dipping
   (such as apples, pears, tangerines,
   grapes, figs, cherries, strawberries
   and kiwi fruit)*

VARIATION

Add a few langues de chat *or
other dessert biscuits, such as
sponge fingers, to the platter.
Children like the yogurt dip
served on its own, with sliced
bananas stirred in.*

Place the yogurt in a dish, beat until smooth, then stir in the honey, swirling it to create a marbled effect.

Cut the fruit into wedges or bite-size pieces, or leave whole.

Arrange the selection of fruits on a platter with the bowl of dip in the centre. Serve chilled.

PEARS WITH HONEY AND WINE

California produces several types of honey, the best known being sage blossom and alfalfa. In this Californian recipe, honey sweetens a mulled wine mixture used for stewing pears.

Serves 4

1 bottle of red Zinfandel wine
175g/6oz/¾ cup granulated sugar
45ml/3 tbsp clear honey
juice of ½ lemon
1 cinnamon stick
1 vanilla pod, split open lengthways,
   or a few drops of vanilla essence
5cm/2in piece of pared orange rind
1 whole clove
1 black peppercorn
4 firm ripe pears
whipped cream or soured cream,
   to serve

In a saucepan just large enough to hold the pears standing upright, combine the wine, sugar, honey, lemon juice, cinnamon stick, vanilla pod or essence, orange rind, clove and peppercorn. Heat gently, stirring occasionally until the sugar has dissolved.

Meanwhile, peel the pears, leaving the core and stem intact on each. Slice a small piece off the base of each pear so that it will stand upright, then gently place the pears in the wine mixture. Simmer the pears uncovered, for 20–35 minutes, depending on size and ripeness. They should be just tender; do not overcook.

With a slotted spoon, gently transfer the pears to a bowl. Continue to boil the poaching liquid until reduced by about half. Leave to cool, then strain over the pears. Chill for at least 3 hours.

Place the pears in serving dishes and spoon over the chilled wine syrup. Serve with whipped cream or soured cream.

COOK'S TIP
Choose pears of similar size and shape for this attractive hot dessert.

Hot Desserts

Friends and family will be buzzing with excitement when you serve these fabulous puddings. Kumquat and honey compote, sweet and creamy rice pudding or fried bananas with honey: every one's a winner!

KUMQUAT AND HONEY COMPOTE

Sun-ripened, warm and spicy ingredients, sweetened with honey, make the perfect winter dessert.

Serves 4

350g/12oz/2 cups kumquats

275g/10oz/1¼ cups dried apricots

30ml/2 tbsp raisins

30ml/2 tbsp lemon juice

1 orange

2.5cm/1in piece of fresh root ginger

4 cardamom pods

4 cloves

30ml/2 tbsp clear honey

15ml/1 tbsp flaked almonds, toasted,

  to decorate

VARIATION

If you prefer, use ready-to-eat dried apricots. Reduce the liquid to 300ml/½pint/1¼cups, and add the apricots for the last 5 minutes of cooking.

Wash the kumquats, and, if they are large, cut them in half. Place them in a large saucepan with the dried apricots and raisins. Pour over 300ml/½ pint/1¼ cups water and add the lemon juice. Bring to the boil.

Pare the rind thinly from the orange and add to the pan. Peel the ginger, grate it finely and add it to the pan. Lightly crush the cardamom pods and add them to the pan, with the cloves.

Lower the heat, cover the pan and simmer gently for about 30 minutes or until the fruit is tender, stirring occasionally.

Squeeze the juice from the orange and add it to the pan with the honey. Stir well, then taste and add more honey if required. Sprinkle with flaked almonds and serve warm.

HONEYED RICE PUDDING

In Spain, Greece, Italy and Morocco rice puddings are a favourite dish, especially when sweetened with honey and flavoured with orange.

Serves 4

50g/2oz/¼ cup short-grain
   pudding rice
600ml/1 pint/2½ cups milk
30–45ml/2–3 tbsp clear honey
finely grated rind of ½ small orange
150ml/¼ pint/⅔ cup double cream
15ml/1 tbsp chopped pistachio nuts,
   toasted, to decorate

COOK'S TIP
It is important to stir the rice pudding regularly to prevent it from sticking to the bottom of the pan.

M ix the rice with the milk, honey and orange rind in a saucepan. Bring to the boil, then lower the heat, cover and simmer very gently for about 1¼ hours, stirring frequently.

Remove the lid and continue cooking and stirring for 15–20 minutes, until the rice is creamy.

Pour in the cream and simmer for 5–8 minutes more. Serve the rice in individual warmed bowls. Sprinkle each portion with pistachio nuts.

FRIED BANANAS WITH HONEY

These delicious treats come from Thailand, where they are sold as snacks throughout the day and night at portable roadside stalls and market places. Honey acts as a delicious instant sweet dipping sauce.

Serves 4

115g/4oz/1 cup plain flour
2.5ml/½ tsp bicarbonate of soda
pinch of salt
30ml/2 tbsp granulated sugar
1 egg
30ml/2 tbsp shredded coconut or
*   15ml/1 tbsp sesame seeds*
4 firm bananas
oil, for frying
mint sprigs and lychees, to decorate
60ml/4 tbsp clear honey, to serve

VARIATION

Any tender but fairly robust fruit can be given this treatment. Pineapple and apple wedges work well.

Sift the flour, bicarbonate of soda and salt together into a mixing bowl. Stir in the granulated sugar. Whisk in the egg and add enough water (about 90ml/6 tbsp) to make quite a thin batter. Whisk in the shredded coconut or sesame seeds.

Peel the bananas, then carefully cut each one in half lengthways, then in half crossways.

Heat the oil in a wok or deep frying pan. Dip the bananas into the batter, then gently drop a few into the oil. Fry until golden brown. Remove from the oil with a slotted spoon and drain on kitchen paper. Decorate with mint sprigs and lychees and serve immediately, with the honey for dipping.

SOUFFLEED RICE AND HONEY PUDDING

The fluffy egg whites make an unusually light rice pudding and the delicate honey flavour brings out its creamy deliciousness.

Serves 4

50g/2oz/¼ cup short-grain
   pudding rice
45ml/3 tbsp clear honey
750ml/1¼ pints/3 cups milk
2.5ml/½ tsp vanilla essence
2 egg whites
5ml/1 tsp freshly grated nutmeg

Place the pudding rice, honey and milk in a heavy or non-stick saucepan and bring the milk to the boil. Lower the heat and cover the saucepan. Simmer gently for about 1–1¼ hours, stirring occasionally to prevent the rice sticking, until most of the liquid has been absorbed. Remove the saucepan from the heat.

Stir in the vanilla essence. Preheat the oven to 220°C/425°F/Gas 7.

Place the egg whites in a clean, dry mixing bowl and whisk them until they hold soft peaks. Using a metal spoon or spatula, fold the egg whites evenly into the pudding rice mixture. Pour into a 1 litre/1¾ pint/4 cup ovenproof dish.

Sprinkle the surface of the rice pudding with plenty of freshly grated nutmeg and bake for 15–20 minutes, until it is well-risen and golden brown. Serve hot.

COOK'S TIP
If you've got one, use a vanilla pod instead of the essence. Add it with the honey and remove it before folding in the egg whites.

INDEX